He Still Speaks

BILL GRIEGO

ISBN 978-1-64191-448-2 (paperback)
ISBN 978-1-64191-449-9 (digital)

Christian Faith Publishing, Inc.
832 Park Avenue
Meadville, PA 16335
www.christianfaithpublishing.com

Printed in the United States of America

Foreword

It is my belief that God desires to talk to His people. He uses many methods to communicate to us. While I do not profess to understand all about the communications that the Holy Spirit uses to communicate to us, I do believe that God has seen fit to give us this collection through the Holy Spirit. It is my sincere hope, that this collection will give the reader a glimpse into the heart of God. At the very least, I pray that it will give hope to the reader. I believe that He gave me each of these poems, many in a time of seeking an answer to a situation I was personally facing. Others came during times of worship, while others were just laid on my spirit at random. It is my belief that I was given each of these for my benefit, but not just for me. I believe that God intended for these to encourage *all* His people. Having said that, it is my sincere prayer that each person who reads this will perceive that God is talking directly to you. It is intended to encourage all who read it.

I never, in my wildest dreams, thought I would ever write a book, much less a book of poetry. It is only after I received confirmation from multiple sources that these poems were meant to be shared, that I agreed to publish them. May God bless each and every one who chooses to buy, or read this book.

I also want to take the time to say to you that God loves you, right where you are, and if you just take the time to "be still and listen," then He will speak to you. It may not be in the way you would expect, but He desires to have a relationship with His people. So I pray that you will enjoy this book and that you will allow God to speak to you through it.

A Song Came to Me

There's a song came to me, out of the dark
That quickened my spirit and pierced through my heart
The music that came down, from heaven above
And brightened my darkness with God's holy love
And the sins that put me in that dark place
Are all now gone, without leaving a trace
Sins that came in like a roaring flood
Are completely gone, washed clean by the blood
So all I did on my own, I mostly did wrong
I can dance in the freedom, because of this song

Breath of God

Breath of God gave life unto me
But in my darkness I failed to see
What the Light of the world did for me
Jesus will help me cope
Even when I turned away
He was there to always say
I will be with you every day
To fill me with unending hope

I was deceived by the enemy
Was blinded, but now I see
God truly cares about me
And will always be by my side
I can see the pain on His face
As, on the cross, He took my place
And, all my sins, He did erase
Made us part of Jesus's bride

Come as You are

Come, come as you are
Come from near, come from afar
Come take hold of my hand
I will meet you where you stand
No matter what you're going through
I will always be there for you
You may succeed, you may fail
But my love, you will prevail
When the enemy's attack comes
Sing the song, beat the drums
Stand and roar just like a lion
Let your strength flow out of Zion

God is Calling

God is calling, ever calling,
Calling us back to Him.
When all seems lost, He paid the cost,
To bring us back to Him.
The child was born, the veil was torn,
All part of the plan.
We can win, freed from sin,
By the Son of Man.
There's no place too far, for the Morning Star,
He'll reach you where you stand
We should shout, as we reach out,
To take His out stretched hand
He will bring you home, from where you roam,
And stand you on your feet
He'll give you a crown, as He smiles down,
From the Mercy Seat
It is perfectly clear
The Lord wants us to hear
What it is He has to say
If we open up our heart
His wisdom He'll impart
He's speaking to us today

You Are Mine

I stood before Your holy hill
And bade my soul to just be still
And tried not to make a sound
As I stood, filled with awe
I can't describe just what I saw
As Your Glory came down
I felt Your mercy and Your grace
And tears ran down my face
Knowing none of this did I earn
Losing all of my own desire
Standing in the refiner's fire
A flame to cleanse, not to burn
The Lord said "Do not be afraid
Or dwell upon mistakes you made
Because you are precious in My sight
When the enemy begins to attack
Know that I got your back
I'll go before you in your fight"
I felt Him smile as He said to me
"Take heart my son, you have the key
It's time to go and let your light shine
You are to be My hands and feet
Overcome challenges you may meet
My Spirit is in you, you are Mine"

King of Glory, King of Grace

King of Glory, King of Grace
How we long to see Your face
Come and fill us in this place
Help us as we run this race
This is where the victory starts
As You fill our soul and hearts
All our guilt and shame departs
As Your presence fills our hearts
You paid the price, once and for all
That tears down the binding wall
Do not let my heart or feet stall
As we heed the Father's call
It's time the world understands
It's time to follow Your commands
This is how You'll heal our lands
As You hold us in Your hands
Since You caused it all to be
I have never felt so free
No longer blind, I now see
Just how much You care for me

Close My Eyes Lord, Let Me See

Close my eyes, Lord, Let me see
The things Your love has for me
Fill my heart with glory that is You
Greater works than these, we will do
You declared it in Your word and we believe
You imparted to us power to declare
Your kingdom on earth, Your Spirit everywhere
We may not always see what You've done
Your glory on our life has only begun
Close my mouth, Lord, that You speak
Let me touch Your face that I seek

Cross the River

I heard the voice of the Lord today
I could hear Him smile as He began to say
"I am here for you, I will never leave
I can do all things, if you just believe
In the face of all your battles, take my hand
In my presence, your enemies just can't stand"
Now I can stand up tall and sing
In the presence of my God and King
It's time for us to take a stand
Cross the river Jordan, to the Promised Land

He Is There In the Storm

Though the storm is raging all around
I will stand tall, I will stand my ground
The work of the cross has set me free
To be all that He called me to be
Set me free to sing a new song
Even when I've done everything wrong
Washed me clean in His own blood
And reached me right where I stood
It's a revelation for me to understand
He desires to protect me with His own hand
His glory shines on me, all around
In His presence, we're on holy ground
Cast your nets out into the deep
The harvest is ripe, it's time to reap
So let it be known to the broken hearted
God will finish all that He started

Freedom We Could Not Have Won

The baby that came from Heaven to earth
To lie in a manger on the night of His birth
He came to take all of our sins away
And to pay the price that was ours to pay
God so loved us, He sent His only Son
To give us freedom, we could not have won
He found you in the fire and He's bringing you through
There's nothing that God cannot do for you

I Can Fulfill Your Every Need

I can fulfill your every need
I can move mountains with lightning fast speed
I can remove all your guilt and shame
If you would just learn to call on my name
I have great gifts for you to receive
All that it takes is for you to believe
I am the way, the truth, and the light
If you would just walk by faith and not sight
All of this was paid for that day on the cross
And you may never understand the full cost
Of the sacrifices for you, that were done
By the love of the Father and of His Son

Lord of Lords

When things aren't going your way
And your joy isn't where it was before
And it seems like the whole world hates you
Jesus said you are worth dying for

Jesus is The Lord of Lords
Jesus is the King of Kings
When I think of Him, my heart leaps
My soul cries out and my spirit sings

Call Out to The Risen Son of Man

Call out to the risen Son of man
His kingdom is at hand
I know that it is true
But surrender all unto the Lord
He's given you His word
He paid the price for you
Believe that the word of God is true
He has done all there is to do
He has atoned for all our sin
We fight the good fight of the Lord
He said it in His word
Through Jesus we will win
We are living in the time of the end
The kingdom of God is at hand
The Lord is calling you by name
He has taken away all of your shame
So rally around the Most High
Now is not the time to be shy
Just like the stories of old
God is calling us to be bold
Call out to the risen Son of man
It's time to take a stand
Let your faith flow like a flood
Give thanks to Jesus Christ, our Lord
It is written in His word
He has saved us by His blood

Open My Heart

As the rain falls from Heaven above
God showers us with His unending love
Until He calls us all to come home
He will never ever leave us alone
God is sounding out His calling
He wants to keep us all from falling
Into the many traps of this world
He gives us strength as the banner's unfurled
Place in me a brand new heart
Take me back to the very start
Bring me close, bring me near
Remove from me any fear
Open up my heart to You
Let me see Your word is true
Let me see as You see above
Filter my vision through Your love

Holy Spirit Calling

Holy Spirit, I hear You calling
My strongholds, I see them falling
It's time for us to go all in
The time is now so quit stalling

It's time we all realize
The enemy loses no matter what he tries
The glory of God will shine in your eyes
When you try the Holy Spirit on for size

I hear His voice, it's crystal clear
Small still voice, yet I still hear
A word that drives away all fear
When you seek Him and draw near

God longs to be close to you
He desires to make all things new
Seek to please Him in all you do
His mercy and grace will pull you through

The Kingdom Is At Hand

Time to take a stand
For the Kingdom is at hand
Strongholds will fall
As we answer God's call
Do not be afraid
As God's power is displayed
The Great I Am has come
All the work is done
This is our greatest hour
As God reveals His power
In our hearts, rejoice
As we listen for His voice
Open your heart and receive
Nothing to do but believe

Promises

The stories were told about the heroes of old
And the promises were made
Well I am here to say, they are all valid today
So you are not to be afraid
Through your glory and strife, God cares about your whole life
He's not just watching from above
So set aside your pride, let Him fight on your side
Our greatest weapon is His love
In the deepest darkest night, and through the fiercest fight
He is there if you only would call
There is never any shame when you need to call His name
With Him we stand, without Him we fall
The hand that holds the stars can take away our scars
And make our broken lives whole
The revelation is clear: when we call, He will hear
And restore what the enemy has stole
He answers every prayer, every time and everywhere
In His name and in His time
So do not be afraid. All the promises that were made
Were given for every place and time

Little Words of Wisdom

These little words of wisdom came to me somehow
You will never be as young as you are right now
I've said all of this to you, just to say
Make the best of what God has given you today
The shame was heaped upon my head
Was completely washed away when Jesus bled
On that faithful day upon that hill
When the Son fulfilled the Father's will
He said "you are human, at times you'll fail
Put your trust in Me and you will prevail"
Sometimes the trials are short, sometimes long
But it's the storms we endure that make us strong

Small Still Voice

There was no thunder from Heaven
No lightning flashing across the sky
No shaking or quaking of the earth
No blinding light shining in my eye
No message on a billboard
No one speaking in my ear
There was just a small, still voice
Only my spirit could hear
The Comforter is there to guide us
If we would learn to hear it
There is wisdom in the word of God
Spoken to us by the Holy Spirit
The kingdom of Heaven brings heaven into earth
The Spirit's here to show us that
To the Father we have worth
All things are possible through
The Holy Spirit living in me
If I surrender my ears to hear
And allow my eyes to see

When the Attack Comes

The attack of the enemy is bordering on the insane
It seems like I'm standing in the middle of a hurricane
Just like the world is falling completely apart
Yet I can smile because God is planted deep in my heart
When things seem impossible, Your banner is unfurled
My treasure lies in heaven, not in the things of this world
When trouble comes a-knocking, and there's no place to hide
The thing we need to remember, God is on our side
Even when the battle is raging all around
Understand you were lost, but you have been found
Even in the depths of darkness, I can sing
I've been redeemed by the Glorious King

Hallelujah King of Grace

Hallelujah, King of Grace
Let Your Spirit fill this place
You will help us run this race
As we strive to seek Your face
As we begin to draw near
You remove all doubt and fear
And restore all that we hold dear
When we welcome Your presence here
Your presence always give us rest
And allows us to do our best
Covers us like an armored vest
Forgives us from the east to west
The end of the age has begun
The battle rages, the war is won
No more to do, it's all been done
On the cross by the Son

Return of Glory

The Lord has come to deliver me from
The mess I've made of my life
He wants us to know that wherever we go
He's taken over our strife
There is nothing we do apart from You
That will help in our time of need
It's the Holy Spirit, if we will hear it
Upon which we need to feed
It's Adam, who fell, that invited hell
Into the very nature of man
But Jesus came to carry the blame
And return God's glory to the land

The Writing Is On The Wall

I can see the writing on the wall
It's time to answer the Father's call
The trumpet sounding loud and clear
Calling out for all to hear
Time to strike up the spark
Bringing light into the dark
Time to take hold of the prize we won
By the sacrifice of the risen Son
Lord, open up our eyes to see
Open up our ears to hear the Word
Bring us to the place we need to be
To walk in the promise that we've heard
Now is the time, today is the day
We will never ever be the same
We will learn to walk a whole new way
By the power of Jesus's name
Lord, put Your fire in my heart
Let Your revival start
Lord, fill us with Your grace
As we seek Your Holy face

Call Out to Christ

Call out, call out to Christ
He is the one who paid the price
God's ultimate sacrifice
Reach out, take His hand
He will meet you where you stand
He will use you, heal your land

Step out of your comfort zone
You don't have to do it on your own
You never have to be all alone
Though you may be in darkest night
Or feel you're always in a fight
Walk in faith, not by sight

His Blessing for You

I spoke with the Lord about you, today
And this is what He had to say
He wants me to say how much He loves you
So much more than even I do
He told me I'm part of His blessing for you
And I told Him, you're a part of my treasure, too

The Lord Is On Our Side

They took Him off the cross
They laid Him in a tomb
But He was not put there to stay
He is risen, the stone's been rolled away

Satan thought he'd won
When they crucified the son
Nailed to a tree the Son of man
Was all part of God's plan
Resurrection from above
Is proof of God's love
The innocence of the Lamb
Was a price paid for man
The Lord is on our side
There is no time left to hide
He is calling you by name
Time to get into the game

Always There

I know that you're scared and that's okay
I'm right here with you, every step of the way
It's not a fight you have to face on your own
I'm always here, you're never alone
When it seems to be the darkest part of the night
Be brave, my child, and become the light
When the going gets rough, and you don't know what to do
Lean on me, I will always bring you through
It's a promise made by paying your cost
That fateful day upon a wooden cross

God Chose You to Be a Mother

God chose you to be a mother
Chose you above all others
The child will teach you love
That comes from the Lord above
A child is an awesome treasure
A show of grace above measure
Even when life hits a hectic pace
You still put a smile on Jesus's face

The Angels in the Room

When I was away, out of town
And the attack sought to strike me down
I was brought back from the edge of doom
Peace was there, the angels were in the room
It was not easy to fight my way back
And get my health back on track
And when all I could see was gloom
I needed to see the angels in the room
The angels were there, each and every day
To guide me on and show me the way
I look out at the flowers in full bloom
And thank God for the angels in the room

Dedicated to the staff at the Heart Hospital Cardiac
Rehab, who were truly the angels in the room.

On That Starry Night

On that starry night, so long ago
Born in Bethlehem town
While shepherds kept their flocks
The angel's glory showed round
For a king is born
Unto you this very day
Wrapped in swaddling clothes
And in a manger lay
For God so loved the world
He gave His only son
That, through His glory and love
The freedom of our soul is won

A Promise

I came, to die upon a tree
I came, to set the captives free
I came, that prophesy'd come true
I came, to do it all for you

I will, always be here for you
I will, always know what to do
I will, promise I will never leave
I will, ask that you only believe

I am, the way, the truth, the light
I am, keeping you in my sight
I am, watching you in love
I am, smiling down from above

There Comes a Time in Every Man's Life

There comes a time in every man's life,
That he must go and choose a wife,
To always be right by his side,
Someone to be his wedded bride.
A woman will become a bride,
And join a husband to stand beside,
No matter what may lie in store,
To love and cherish forever more.
Together they will go forth,
And live life, for all it's worth,
Through good and bad, better, or worse,
For you, I have prepared this little verse.
Today, two have become one.
Your life together has now begun.
When life comes at you helter skelter
Remember, you are each other's shelter

Not Us, You

Yea though I walk through the valley of the shadow of death
You sustain us through the battle with Your very breath
When the world seems to be gaining the upper hand
Upon Your word is where we all need to stand
You take away our sorrow, You take away our shame
You take away our hurting, through the power of Your name
You never will forsake us, never ever let us down
It will never be in our strength that we receive our crown
Your love is always with us, it will never ever end
It always blows my mind, that You have called me friend
When it comes to our mistakes, You never do keep score
You have forgiven us, for now, forever, and forevermore

When We Listen

Give me eyes to see, give me ears to hear
Lord, let me feel Your heart
The trumpet sounds, the call goes out
Lord, I want to do my part
The grapes are on the vine, ready for new wine
The time for harvest is near
The time has truly come, the victory is won
The Kingdom of Heaven is here
Let the weary have rest, God gives us His best
Take refuge in His word
You have everything to gain when you let God reign
And let Him be your Lord
When we renew our mind, the truth we will find
When we listen for His voice
God keeps on calling, strongholds keep on falling
It's time we make our choice
When we answer His call and surrender all
His mercy and grace we find
If we just stand still and let Him do His will
Our healing we will find

Prodigal

Lord, we know we've gone astray
Forgive us now for drifting away
Help us now to come back home
You never ever left us alone
Fill us, Lord, change our heart
Help us, Lord, to do our part
Wandering is destroying our land
Now is the time to rise and stand
Time for us to make the shift
Drop our anchor, stop our drift
When we attach our lives to You
You will make old things new
So bless the Lord, oh my soul
And give the Father complete control
When we return, like prodigal sons
He will finish what He has begun

Overcome

We need to move from surviving
Into a place of truly thriving
Even when it is raining
We need to quit complaining
When you are in the time of lack
And you are under attack
Get up, start to dance and sing
For you are a child of the true King
Many of our times of winning
Began with a small beginning

Rise Up In The Name Of the Lord

Rise up in the name of the Lord
Swing wide the double-edged sword
The time has come to fight
In the Spirit that is right

Satan will surely see
Any weakness in me
And will bring his attack
Upon that very lack

The fire started with a spark
Then brought light into the dark
In that light I finally see
The gift Jesus gave is free

We were given back what we lost
Jesus paid the full cost
The Lord is lifting off our veil
So we can see His spirit will prevail

Greater Works

Jesus arose right out of the grave
After giving His all for the world to save
He has deemed us worthy, it's nothing we have done
It's because of His great love, He offered up His son
Jehovah Jireh, You have made a way
For us to be in Your presence, each and every day
It's time for me to take my strongholds off the shelf
We have to free ourselves from the trappings of our minds
It is His righteousness, sight given to the blind
Great miracles He did, and all the world still sees
But Jesus said to me, you'll do greater works than these

Unending

Let me tell you a story
About God's unending glory
And how He fills our souls
It is a true healing
Not just a feeling
When you're giving Him control
Before the battle had begun
The victory was won
But we still must fight the fight
So remember all you heard
And rely upon the Word
Because it will bring you to the light
When my faith began to fail
Started walking through my own hell
I lost sight of God's unending grace
God won't leave you all alone
Won't leave you on your own
He is with you to the end of this race

Feed the Sheep

There's a truth told to me
Took me a long time to see
I thought, how could this be?
God is crazy about me
Jesus stretched out His hand
To reach me where I stand
He said, "I will heal your land"
Thank God, I finally understand
Jesus came in the middle of my night
Even though I put up quite a fight
Opened my eyes, He gave me sight
Covered my sin, made me right
Time to awaken from our sleep
Go into the world and feed His sheep
Cast our nets out into the deep
All God's promises, He will keep

Trials and Triumph

The ground is shaking, the earth is quaking
There is uncertainty everywhere
But God is calling, strongholds are falling
There is a promise in the air
The time is here, a change is near
Get ready to receive
The world is lost, but He paid the cost
You only need to believe
All the trials, and all the smiles
Are only for a season
All the things that you are walking through
Are for a good reason
The things we bear, are to prepare
Us for much greater things
Now that we know, this is how we grow
You can have the joy God brings

The Prize

Sitting here in the middle of all my trials and troubles
Looking at them, it's as if they multiply by double
When the water is too deep and I feel like I will drown
I hold on tight to the One that won't let me down
When I am tired, and the finish line seems so very, very far
I can't do this alone, I have to cling to the real Morning Star

But when I lift up my eyes
And look to the real prize
My troubles melt away
He will dry up our tears
And calm all our fears
And reveal the light of day

And when I am lost in the wilderness, and can't find a way out
Sometimes the noise is so deafening, I can't hear myself shout
Looking at my problems, seems like everything is uphill
He will help us through it all, if we just rest and be still

Small Voice in the Storm

When the lightning strikes and the thunder rolls
And it seems that, in everything, I have lost control
There remains one thing that is constant and true
When I have lost everything else, I can always count on You
No matter how much I make a mess of things
You give my heart a million reasons to relax and sing
When life takes me on a roller coaster ride
I have to look to the One who lives inside
I have to make a clear and conscious choice
To listen closely to Your small still voice
Even if times are tough, You will not leave me in lack
You are always there, You have my back

He's My Dad

He's my dad, I shout it loud
I only hope I've made him proud
The things he's said and the things he's done
Has helped make me the man I've become
He is as honest as anyone can be
And worked harder than a worker bee
He provided for us even if he did without
Father of the year? For me, there is no doubt
He did his best to keep us in line
A better dad, you will not find
Thank you for all that you have done
From my heart, your loving son

Take Me Back

Invasion, it's happening today
The enemy, is not here to play
Rebellion, it's only the start
It's poison, to weaken your heart
Place in me a brand-new heart
Take me back to the very start
Bring me close, bring me near
Remove from me any fear
Open up my heart to You
Let me see Your word is true
Let me see as You see above
Filter my vision through Your love

Call upon the name of the Lord

Call upon the name of the Lord, your God;
Call upon the name of the Lord!
When all seems lost and you cannot cope,
Call upon the name of the Lord!
He is the one who will give you hope,
Call upon the name of the Lord!
When troubles come and all seems lost,
Call upon the name of the Lord!
Cry out to the one who paid the cost,
Call upon the name of the Lord!
When the enemy is coming from all around,
Call upon the name of the Lord!
Victory is yours, hear the trumpet sound,
When you call upon the name of the Lord.
When everything is wrong and nothing's right,
Call upon the name of the Lord!
Call out to Him, He will fight your fight,
Call upon the name of the Lord!
Call upon the name of the Lord, your God;
Call upon the name of the Lord!

I Said a Prayer

I said a prayer for you, today
A prayer like many others
Though you moved a thousand miles away
You know you're still my brother
I asked the Lord to give you strength
To endure all that you'll go through
He smiled at me and then He winked
And said, I know just what to do
He said to me, I know your heart
And for this friend, it breaks
I've always been there from the start
And I'll do all that it takes
To see them through their trials
And bring joy to their life
And fill their home again with smiles
Because they are precious in my sight

This Is Christmas

This is Christmas
A time for family, a time for friends
A time for Joy that never ends
The greatest gift from God above
Of His son, Jesus, and His love
The events set in motion that very night
Would bring the deaf hearing, to the blind, sight

About the Author

Bill Griego was born in the late 1950s in the small rural town of Dalhart, Texas. He grew up in Dalhart and graduated from Dalhart High school. He grew up playing football throughout junior high and high school, though not well enough to play in college. He spent one year at Angelo State University in San Angelo, Texas. Rock and roll has always played an important role in his life, at least in his mind. After spending another year back in Dalhart, he moved to the Dallas, Texas area to attend electronics school. After that, he spent several years working in the defense contractor industry. Then he learned phone and data cabling, eventually ending up at a major telecommunications company, where he currently works in the IT department.

He married his wife of twenty-six years, Judy, and they became a family that now consists of five children, thirteen grandchildren, and seven great-grandchildren. He enjoys going on mission trips to Cambodia, where he and his wife have been five times. His hobbies are playing golf, riding motorcycles, and playing with his great grand-children. He also helps with the sound department at his church. He and his wife, are part of the leadership team of their church, which they have been attending for twenty years. Writing poetry is a God-given talent that, through encouragement from family and friends, led to this book.

CPSIA information can be obtained
at www.ICGtesting.com
Printed in the USA
FSHW04n0558120418
46623FS